INSPIRATIONAL ENCOURAGEMENT

STAY THE COURSE

God is Making Something Beautiful in His Time

ECCLESIASTES 3:11

JANET VIERS

Limits of Liability and Disclaimer of Warranty

The author and publisher shall not be liable for your misuse of this material. This book is strictly for informational and educational purposes. The purpose of this book is to educate and entertain. The author and/or publisher do not guarantee that anyone following these techniques, suggestions, tips, ideas, or strategies will become successful. The author and/or publisher shall have neither liability nor responsibility to anyone with respect to any loss or damage caused, or alleged to be caused, directly or indirectly by the information contained in this book.

Views expressed in this publication do not necessarily reflect the views of the publisher.

Printed in the United States of America

ISBN 978-0-9987200-9-8

Keen Vision Publishing, LLC

www.keen-vision.com

ACKNOWLEDGEMENTS

First and foremost, I give all Glory to God for inspiring and strengthening me to complete this book. I am so honored that You chose me for the assignment of encouraging your people.

I would like to acknowledge my family: my husband, John; my daughter, Johnetta; my son, John; and my grandchildren, Katilyn, Jaida, and Jackson.

I would like to thank my siblings for their support and prayers throughout the years, my sisters: Bertha Jones, Kathleen Anderson, Annie Newman, Marilyn Davis and Orean Edwards, adopted sister, Christine Clay, (deceased, Rosie Davis, Gladiolus Clay and Jacqueline Lee); and my brothers, George Lightfoot, Thomas Lightfoot, Willie Lightfoot, Melton Lightfoot and Elton Lightfoot. (deceased: Lermis Lightfoot and Michael Hollins) as well as all of their husbands and wives. I love each of you.

To Orean, my baby sister, Thank you for being my secretary, my proofreader, my supporter and my friend. Sister LaRosa (Kaye) Davis, thank you for being my early morning prayer partner for almost two years concerning my book and other assignments. Bishop Ernest Clay, my pastor, and First Lady Christine Clay, thank you for your prayers and support. I would like to express my appreciation to my church family, The Living Way Apostolic Church, Town Creek, Alabama.

To my sister Orean Edwards, my daughter Johnetta Viers, my husband, John Viers and my niece Reshina Powell, thank you for proofreading my manuscript. Your help will never go unnoticed. First Lady Christine Clay, thank you for designing my book cover. Finally, I would like to thank everyone involved with Women Inspiring Women Ministry. You ladies have inspired me in so many ways.

DEDICATION

I would like to dedicate this book to John, my loving husband. I'm so blessed to be married to such a wonderful man for 34 years and counting. It would take another book to tell how when he found me and made me his wife, he found a good thing and obtained favor. You are truly a man that has always provided for your family. Most of all, your love for God has brought our family through many tests and trials. Thank you for teaching me how to wait on God by staying focused and staying the course. I also, thank God for the late Ms. Celeste J. Briscoe, who gave birth to this wonderful man and his father, Mr. Jack Viers. I love you, John Viers! Thank you for loving me!

I would also like to dedicate this book to My (deceased) Sister, Gladiolus Clay. Thank you for being my guardian after our parents died. You were the epitome of a godly woman who led by example, in living a clean and sanctified life. Through your love and dedication to God, you were my role model to become the woman I am today. Although you encountered a lot of sickness and pain in your latter years, I never saw you lose your Praise to God. You were a strong woman of God. I salute you for the example you lived before me and others. When life tests and trails get hard to bear, I can reflect on your steadfast love and determination to make this journey. It gives me the strength I need to go a little farther. My sister, you will forever hold a special place in my heart. I love and miss you so much my guardian, my sister. You can't come to me, but if I continue to stay the course, I can come to you. Love you, Sis! Also, thank you Bishop Earnest Clay for allowing my sister to let me come and live with you all. You are very special to me. I love you so much.

ABOUT THE AUTHOR

"He that dwelleth in the secret place of the most High shall abide under the shadow of the Almighty."

Psalm 91:1 (KJV)

Meet Janet Lightfoot Viers. She is a native of Courtland, Alabama, and currently resides in Decatur, Alabama. She is the mother of two children and three grandchildren. Janet and her groom, John Viers, have enjoyed 34 beautiful years of marital bliss. Janet has been a member of The Living Way Apostolic Church for over 30 years.

Though this is her first book, Janet is no stranger to encouraging others. She has spoken at many empowering women conferences. Janet is a behind-the-scenes servant of God who enjoys lending a helping hand to others.

She is the founder of Women Inspiring Women Ministries, a non-profit organization that equips women to pursue their dreams. The motto of WIW is "Every woman has a story, and when they are ready, they will share it!" This motto perfectly fits the life of Author Janet Viers. She has an amazing story of trials and tribulations that she uses to glorify God and encourage and build His Kingdom. From her life experiences, Janet has learned that God makes everything beautiful in its time. Her many tests and trials have taught her that God is faithful and steadfast.

Janet's goal is to mentor and encourage others on their walk in purpose. Her greatest strength is her love for God, family, and her love for His people. Her latest book, Stay the Course, is designed to inspire and encourage people from all walks of life. Though this is her first book, this certainly won't be the last book we read from Janet Viers. Janet is on a mission to ensure that the Kingdom of God is never without encouragement and an extra push! She strives to leave a legacy for the next generation.

CONTENTS

INTRODUCTION

"He hath made every thing beautiful in his time: also he hath set the world in their heart so that no man can find out the work that God maketh from the beginning to the end."
Ecclesiates 3:11(KJV)

When life hits, it hits hard. We often find ourselves in situations and circumstances that literally knock the breath out of us. When we are faced with these difficult challenges, we sometimes don't know what to do or where to turn. It often feels like as soon as we take care of one thing, something else goes completely haywire. During these times, it's easy to feel like giving up, throwing in the towel, or running away.

Like many of you reading this book, I've experienced my share of trials and tribulations. I understand how tough things can get. I wrote this book to encourage you to stay the course, no matter what life may throw at you. For quite some time, I desired to write a book. I didn't just want to write any book. I wanted to write a book that would encourage, empower, and uplift God's people. After much prayer and supplication, God released me to write this book for such a time as this.

I know you may be thinking, "Lady, you don't know anything about my life. How can you tell me to stay the course? Do you have any idea how difficult this is?" The truth is, I may not know you personally, but I know God personally. His word promises that He will make things beautiful in His time. For this reason, I know that your latter shall be greater and that whatever you are dealing with does not compare to the amazing things that are on the way.

To stay the course means to stand firm in pursuing a goal or course of action and to persevere in the face of whatever challenges or obstacles one may encounter. It means that no matter what trials, tribulations, or temptations we may endure, we remain on the course God has set for us.

Before we dig in, I want to provide you with a few principles that are important as you stay the course.

HAVE FAITH. BE COURAGEOUS. TRUST GOD.

As we stay the course in which God has set for us, we must do so with total trust and confidence in God and His Word. Scripture tells us that we must walk by faith, and not by sight. It is sometimes difficult for us to walk by faith, because faith is not based on what we see, rather what we believe in our hearts according to the

Word of God. Every attack from the enemy is designed to kill our faith. The enemy knows that if we don't have faith, it would be difficult for us to please God. God allows the attacks from the enemy to strengthen our faith. Through the enemy's attacks, God allows us to see that though the weapons may form, they will not prosper. He allows them so that we will see that no matter what we go through, He is always there to protect us, provide for us, and ensure that everything works out on our behalf. When we allow ourselves to look at the attacks that often hit our lives from this angle, we can trust God even more. Make no mistake, trusting God can be a little shaky at times. For this reason, we must be courageous enough to do the difficult things He instructs us to do even when it doesn't make sense.

We must trust God enough to not deviate from the path that He has us on, even when the path may not be clear. Even though we might not always understand His Ways, it is imperative that we trust His Word. It is difficult to trust something that you are not familiar with, so we must make prayer and reading the Bible a consistent part of our daily lives.

COMMIT YOUR HANDS TO DO GOOD WORKS.

In addition to trusting God, we must also keep our flesh under subjection to His Word. 1 John 2:15-17(KJV) says:

"Love not the world, neither the things that are in the world. If any man love the world, the love of the Father is not in him. For all that is in the world, the lust of the flesh, and the lust of the eyes, and the pride of life, is not of the Father, but is of the world. And the world passeth away, and the lust thereof: but he that doeth the will of God abideth for ever."

Worldly things can only provide temporary pleasure. They may feel good for the moment, however, that great feeling is soon to pass. If we truly desire to be satisfied and fulfilled, we must commit our hands to do the good works God has commanded us to do. Our focus in life should not be acquiring more money, being popular, or building a platform for ourselves. Matthew 6:33 reminds us that when we seek the Kingdom of God first, everything else is added to it.

YOU MUST OBEY AND SUBMIT.

In many instances, the Bible speaks of God's desire for our obedience and submission. If we want to do anything or be anybody for God, the Word reminds us that we must first be obedient and submitted to God's Will. In addition to being submitted and obedient to God, we must also submit to the pastor He has sent to us. Having a spiritual covering is a vital key to staying the course. Our pastor is the individual in which God has selected to shepherd us. Jeremiah 3:15 (KJV) says, "And I will give you pastors according to mine heart, which shall feed you with knowledge and understanding." To be in right standing with God and be prosperous in our course, we must be obedient and submit to the pastor God has given us according to His own heart. Our Pastor's role in our lives is to feed us with knowledge and understanding. In moments when we don't have clarity, they are there to support us, pray for us, and provide wise counsel. For this reason, we must remember to submit to them. We must also remember that they are not God, however, they speak the words in which God has instructed them to speak.

  Stay the Course was written to be an aide and a source of encouragement for those uncertain times we often experience. I pray that this book empowers you to keep pushing and serving God with your whole heart no matter your situation. Believe by faith that you will come through every storm victoriously! No matter what, know that God will get the Glory out of every situation. Finally, I encourage you to remember to Stay the Course. God is making things beautiful in His time. Are you ready to start this journey with me? Well, turn the page and let's begin.

Chapter One
WE ARE GOD'S WORKMANSHIP

"For ye are bought with a price: therefore, glorify God in your body, and in your spirit, which are God's."

1 Corinthians 6:20 (KJV)

I f you've never asked yourself these questions, take a moment to do so now. Who are you? What were you created to do? Understanding these questions allows us to get in alignment with God's Plan for our lives. When we know why we were created and what we were created to be, we can better understand why we must stay the course.

WHO AM I?

Ephesians 2:10 (KJV) says, "For we are his workmanship, created in Christ Jesus unto good works, which God hath before ordained that we should walk in them." In this scripture, Paul refers to us as God's workmanship.Merriam-Webster defines workmanship as something affected, made or produced; and, the art or skill of a workman. Have you ever seen an artist at work? As they work, they pay very close attention to what they are doing. They are intentional about the entire process. They take pride in their work, and they handle it with care. In Ephesians 2:10, Paul reminds us that we are God's workmanship. On the sixth day of creation, God created us. He crowned us with glory and honor and gave us dominion over all the Earth. Isn't that amazing? Among all the creations He made, He chose us to have dominion over them all. We are fearfully and wonderfully made. God designed us just the way He wanted us to be. He was so intentional in creating us that He knows the number of hairs that are on our heads. We may not be special to a lot of people, but we are special to God. He created us with a purpose, a plan, and a course. Because He is such a loving Father, He also gave us everything we would need to stay the course He has chosen for us.

I don't know about you, but it makes me feel pretty special to know that God put so much work into creating me. Sometimes in life, we can experience situations that cause us not to see how valuable we are. Who we are is not determined by how much money we have, how many people know us, or our job title. Who we are is defined by what God says about us in His Word. God's love for us is beyond our understanding. The Bible tells us that He loves us so much, that He gave His Son to die for our sins. Think about that for just a moment. Would you give up your child for the life of another? Most people wouldn't. God's love for us is perfect. The way He loves us is what defines us. His Love for us gives us our value. We are the offspring of God. It is through Him that we live, move, breathe and are living! Everything we are is because of God, not ourselves or other people. Since God is our Creator and make our lives possible, we shouldn't look to anything or anyone else to define us. To stay the course, we must choose to believe what God has to say about us, rather than what people have to say. When we look at the sovereignty of God and understand His creative power, which we find in His Word, we will understand who we are.

WHAT AM I CREATED TO DO?

When we think about what we were created to do, we instantly think about a job, career, or business. While God has gifted us with skills and talents to do amazing things, this is not the base of what we were created to do. Matthew 6:33 tells us to first seek the Kingdom of God. In everything we do, our focus should be to please God and live righteously. Let's take a moment and talk about what God has created us to do.

When we were in the world, we did what we wanted to do and how we wanted to do it. When we give our life to Christ, we are no longer our own. We must live the way He has called us to live. Why? Because we have been bought with the price of His Blood. 1 Corinthians 6:20 (KJV) says, *"For ye are bought with a price: therefore, glorify God in your body, and in your spirit, which are God's."* Since Christ purchased us with His blood, our job is to glorify Him with our lives. We were created to enjoy God forever and to be delighted in knowing Him. We were created to serve, worship, honor, and glorify God in our spirit, soul, and body. We do this by the way we live, our mannerisms, actions, and character. We were created to love God with all our heart and to love one another as ourselves. God created us to live a life that pleases Him and to produce good fruit. Christ has invested in us His Spirit to lead and guide us into all truth. He created us to be a light to this dying world. God created us to be different. By giving our lives to the will of God, we are put on a path. Our paths are uniquely determined by God. He did not intend for us to be alike, but to be like-minded in Christ. Philippians 2:2 (KJV) says, *"Fulfil ye my joy, that ye be likeminded, having the same love, being of one accord, of one mind."* The Bible tells us that each of our functions is different, but we all are connected to one body.

As dear children of God, we are created to serve God and help one another. As helpers in the body of Christ, every one of us were created to serve in the kingdom of God. God chose us before the foundation of the Earth to serve and worship Him with our whole lives. When we think about the mistakes we've made, it's hard to believe that God still loves us the way He does. It's hard to believe that He still trust and expect so much from us.

John 1:12 (KJV) says, *"But as many as received Him, to them gave He power to become the sons of God, even to them that believe on His name."* This lets us know that once we receive Christ and believe in Him, God gives us the power to be righteous. We are no longer a slave to sin, but a child of the King. We are redeemed, forgiven, and set free from sin. We are the heirs of the Almighty God. The Bible says that we are new creatures in Christ and old things have passed away. Therefore, we are no longer our own, we have been purchased by the blood of Jesus. The mistakes we made in the past doesn't matter anymore. When we repent, He forgives us of our sins and casts them as far as the east is from the west.

Though we might not always feel whole, we have been made complete in Christ Jesus. Therefore, we are bold and confident through faith in Christ Jesus! We are holy, and our life is hidden in Christ Jesus because He has chosen us. Therefore, no matter how many times we mess up, we must repent, stay the course, and allow God to bring out the beauty in us.

If we move into the direction God is leading us, we will go forth and be soul winners for Christ. God has empowered us to live according to His word, and our fruit should remain within us. Of course, the devil does not want the kingdom of God to move forward, so he entices us with the works of our flesh, such as pride, envy, jealousy, and other fleshly desires. We cannot allow pride to set up within us. Pride takes us off the course God has us on. In 1 John 3:2, The Apostle John tells us that we are the sons of God, and this takes place through a transformation process. These words encourage us to continue the course. Right now, it does not appear what we shall be, so we must continue pressing forward on the right path. Also, Apostle John gives us the Word of God to inspire us to live pure lives before God.

Above all else, we were created to love God and to love one another. We are to abide in God's word and keep His commandments by His Spirit whom He has given to us. Therefore, we know when He appears, we shall be like Him, for we shall see Him as He is. Oh, what a Glorious day to look forward to!

You might have been told by someone that you are nobody based on who your parents are or possibly because of the things you have done in life. Perhaps you had a child out of wedlock, or maybe you have been to jail or prison. Maybe you were an alcoholic, drug addict, or even a drug dealer. Maybe you were a cheater, fornicator, or an adulterer. The list goes on. No matter what your past may look like, stay the course, my friend. The Word of God says in Romans 3:23 that we all have sinned and come short of the glory of God. We are not like the Almighty God who had no sin. Each one of us was born into sin and shaped in iniquity, but it took Christ's precious blood to redeem us. Don't be intimidated by where someone else is in life. Remember they had a beginning just like you. Don't fret or covet anyone else's journey. God designed our pathway just for us because He know what is within us and see our expected end.

Somewhere along your life journey, someone may have told you that you were worthless. They may have told you that you wouldn't amount to much. They may have even called you ugly, weird, dumb, crazy, etc. I'm here to tell you today that all of that is a lie. You are the workmanship of God. As we stay the course God has selected for us, we must not allow the world to define who we are.

As we yield ourselves to God, we give Him full range to make us perfect in Him. God began a work in us to make us usable for the kingdom. The Bible tells us that He will continue that work! No matter how many mistakes we make, God won't give up on us. He will keep working with us, in us, and through us. God created us, so He knows who we are even when we are in our worst state. As we journey through this life and understand the sovereignty of God, it will become more apparent why we should stay the course.

Chapter Two
EVERYONE HAS A COURSE

"Jesus, Jesus, precious Jesus! Oh, for grace to trust Him more!"
Louisa M.R. Stead

One of my favorite songs, "Tis So Sweet to Trust in Jesus" was written in 1882 by Louisa M. R. Stead. What I find even more inspiring is the story behind the song. According to the story, one beautiful sunny day, Louisa M. Stead, her husband, and her daughter Lily decided to go on a picnic. They went picnicking on Long Island Sound. While on their picnic, the Steads heard a scream. It was a young boy drowning in the water nearby. Mr. Stead ran to his rescue. Louisa Stead and young Lily watched helplessly as Mr. Stead and the boy drowned. Their troubles were not over yet. Without her husband, Mrs. Stead became very poor and destitute. Yet, God never left her. He provided for her always, and she and her daughter made it through. Louisa learned to trust God, and wrote the words to the song "Tis So Sweet to Trust in Jesus." Shortly after this incident, Louisa and her daughter, Lily, moved to South Africa where they became missionaries. Now, this song is included in many hymnals and has been recorded by many artists.

On this journey, we must learn to trust God with everything within us. As we draw close to God, He will draw close to us. We will learn who He really is and how much He loves and cares about us. God desires to reveal the beauty of this walk with Him. As we walk with Him, He will open the Scriptures to us through the Spirit of wisdom and revelation. He will reveal to us His deep love for us that we can only find in Him.

Proverbs 3:5-7 (KJV) says, *"Trust in the Lord with all thine heart; and lean not unto thine own understanding. In all thy ways acknowledge him, and he shall direct thy paths. Be not wise in thine own eyes: fear the Lord, and depart from evil."* Tragedy sometimes happens in our lives to see if we will remain faithful to God. The devil's job is to try to throw us off course and cause us to doubt God. Don't let him. He is the father of lies. To stay on course, we must stay close to God. We stay close to God by studying and applying the Word in our everyday walk. Communication is the biggest key in any relationship. When my husband and I got married, we were instructed always to keep an open line of communication in our marriage. That piece of advice might seem insignificant to a good marriage, but I promise it is very vital for a healthy marriage. This advice is even more important for our relationship with God.

Out of pain, Louisa M. R. Stead birthed the words, "Tis so sweet to trust in Jesus, just to take Him at His Word." Can you imagine being in her shoes? Losing her husband, struggling to make ends meet, grieving, and still having to be a mother was no doubt a difficult experience for her. Sometimes, life circumstances bring us a lot of pain and disappointment, but when we build a relationship with God and understand His word, then we understand that everything we endure is a part of His designed purpose for us.

On this journey, there will always be some suffering. God's Word says in 2 Timothy 2:12 (KJV), *"If we suffer, we shall also reign with him: if we deny him, he also will deny us."* To stay the course, we must develop a prayer life and pray with belief, confidence, and trust in the Almighty God. We must trust God in everything. One of the sayings of the late Mother Gladiolus Clay was, *"BELIEVE! Because Emanuel lives, I expect victory every time!"* She said these words with much faith and confidence, and I saw God move in a mighty way.

On this path, some of us will experience sickness, financial issues, family issues, job issues, home issues, and even church issues. Nevertheless, we must stay on track because God is making something beautiful out of every situation. When we go through tough trials, it is for God's Glory. The devil is always looking for an opportunity to discredit the children of God testimonies. Even when we got off course and headed in the wrong direction, God was able to steer us back to the right path. Also, God has intercessors in the body of Christ to cry out unto Him to hold back His judgment and for us to get back on course.

Everybody has a unique path. It is up to each of us to choose the right direction. One of my most favorite chapters in the Bible is Romans 12. In Romans 12, Paul reminds us to present ourselves as a living sacrifice to God. As foreigners in this land, we must not allow ourselves to conform to the ways of the world. We are here to be a light to the world. It will be impossible for us to be a light if we are doing and thinking the same way as the world. Paul tells us to be transformed by the renewing of our mind. It is only with a renewed mind that we can understand the good and perfect will of God. In Romans 12, Paul warns us to be sober-minded, and not to think more of ourselves than we ought. This chapter is filled with so much practical information, but for this chapter, I want us to focus solely on verses 4-5. Romans 12:4-5 says, *"For as we have many members in one body, and all members have not the same office: So we, being many, are one body in Christ, and every one members one of another."*

God has called each of us to do something different in the body of Christ. As we understand more about who God is and what He has called us to do, He will begin to reveal our specific assignments and tasks. Though we all have different tasks, each of our tasks work together to build up the Kingdom of God. For us to lift up Christ here on the Earth, we must all do our part to impact the Kingdom, according to our measure of faith. Paul says that each man is given according to His faith. Whatever our God-given talents or assignment may be, we must work at it with all our hearts. We must work unto the glory of God. We cannot allow ourselves to waste time thinking about who will get recognition or praise. We must make sure that we are doing our part no matter who pat us on the back or say, "Job well done!" Our goal and focus should be to glorify God in the way He has instructed us to do.

When we all do our part, stay in our lane, and focus on our course, things run so much smoother! The world is supposed to look to the body of Christ to be the standard as to how they should live. It is impossible for us to be the standard if we are not doing our part. The main focus of this chapter is that you understand that we all have a course. It is up to us to choose to follow it.

To stay the course, we must strive to be more like Christ. How can we be more like Christ? Well, it is very easy to read the scriptures, but sometimes it is hard to live by the scriptures we read. We must understand we cannot do it through the working of our flesh. The only way we can be more Christ-like is through Christ! Though it may seem difficult, Philippians 4:13 reminds us that we can do all things through Christ who strengthens us!

One of the most important ways we can be more Christ-like is by loving others. Because we all have a course to follow, we must remember to love one another. Life can be tough. The last thing we need is to be treated badly by our brothers and sisters. This happens so often in the body of Christ, and it is heartbreaking. As Christians, God has instructed us to love everyone. He did not say, "Love those who do right by you," or "Only love those who are in your circle." He told us to love ALL people. Before we can do that, we must see people as God sees people. God looks at people differently than we do. God understand their entire life and history. He knows every thought, motive, and feeling. He knows how they have changed over time. Most importantly, God see their hearts and souls. He knows their ending from their beginning. When we look at others, we only see who they are at the moment. How can we pass judgment and criticism on people we barely know? We shouldn't. For this reason, God warns us in His Word not to judge others. Sometimes, we think we know everything, but God won't let us know everything because of pride. Once we get in tune with the Holy Ghost and see people as God sees them, we cannot help but to sympathize, understand, and love them.

When we have genuine love for God, we will have a fervent love for His people because God is love. Jesus love heals broken hearts, builds bridges, brings hope, and changes one's life. When we see the good in everyone, we learn to respect and love each person we encounter. Love, friendship, and trust brings out the best in everyone. Dismissing, rejecting, ignoring and disrespecting a person brings out the worst in them…and in us. When we look for the good in others and treat each person with respect, we can help our brothers and sisters blossom. Jesus' love brings the best out of every one of us. Jesus' love brings back the honesty, love, and trust of the children we once were. Jesus' love changes our hearts. Jesus' love makes all the difference. God knows what each of us is capable of. Therefore, He knows the course to put us on. He knows what is needed to build character in us and bring us unto His expected end. God is too wise to make a mistake. Stay the course, God is at work on our behalf.

Chapter Three
GOD IS STILL IN CHARGE

"God is our refuge and strength, an ever-present help in trouble."

Psalm 46:1(KJV)

Sometimes, we act as if God does not know about the things that are going on in our lives. My friend, God always knows exactly where we are within our minds and intellect. Jeremiah 29:11 (KJV) says, *"For I know the thoughts that I think toward you, saith the Lord, thoughts of peace, and not of evil, to give you an expected end."* Like many of us, the prophet Jeremiah went through many trials and tribulations. Many times, these trials and tribulations caused him to cry out to God. Jeremiah often felt as if God had left Him or forgotten about Him. Like many of us, Jeremiah often doubted if he could make it through his dark times. In Jeremiah 29:11, God consoled Jeremiah by reminding Jeremiah that He was God. In so many words, God said, *"Look, son. I know what I think toward you. I AM GOD! I am not going to harm you. I created you. I love you. I wrote your life story. I AM all wise and all knowing. I do not make mistakes. I know what is best for you."* In our times of trouble, God whispers these same words to us.

I know it does not make sense when trouble is all around us. Sometimes, it seems as if it will destroy us. If we know what God's Word says, then the trials and tests would make perfect sense. As we go through the process of being made in His image, the word tells us in John 15:2 (KJV), *"Every branch in me that beareth not fruit He taketh away: and every branch that beareth fruit He purgeth it, that it may bring forth more fruit."* You see, God sees and knows things about us that need to be purged out of us so we can bear more fruit and that the fruit would remain. There is a purpose in everything God allows us to go through. When it does not make sense, we need to just trust in His word. Even though we say we believe that God is great and has all power, our actions don't always line up with what our mouths say. For this reason, we continue to be discouraged and defeated. We must trust God's Word and stand on it until He gives us our expected end. When God brings us into our expected end, He will no longer call us a servant, but HE will call us friend, and make known to us what the Father has spoken concerning us! John 15:15 (KJV) GLORY!

As I travel back in my mind, I remember some things that did not make sense to me. My mother died when I was only seven-years-old. Losing my mother at such a young age was difficult. I felt particularly sad on the first days of school when we were asked to tell about our families. I would talk about my father and my siblings, but I could not talk about my mother. I would sit and listen as all the other children talked about their mothers and fathers. They seemed to have the perfect family. I remember being so sad that I didn't have both parents. I did not understand how God could take a little girl's mother away from her at such a young age.

Year after year, I would go through the same torture. After some time had passed, God allowed my father to remarry. As a young girl, I was happy to have a stepmother I could talk about at school. Life picked up and began moving forward again for me. Then along came another confusing and heartbreaking moment. When I was fifteen, my father passed away. The pain of facing life without my dad was hard. At that time, I did not understand why a child should have to go through so much pain so early in life. During those moments, I experienced a lot of pain that I did not know how to release. I would go in my bedroom, sing sad songs, and cry because I did not understand. I did not know where I belonged. Now that I am mature in Christ, I can look back and realize that God was making something beautiful out of my life and it was going to happen in His time.

When we experience moments like this, we often don't know how to channel the pain. Sometimes we take our frustration and hurt out on others. I know because I've been there. During these times, we must reach out to God for the help we need. We cannot justify going through life blaming our parents, siblings, family members, preachers, or even the church for our mishaps in life. We must understand that this journey called life will bring hard moments. In the midst of it all, we must trust our Maker and release our frustration into His hands.

Even as God's people, we tend to forget who our Maker is. Therefore, when we go through trying times, we look to everyone and everything before we look to God. Some of us trust in our jobs, the government, doctors, lawyers, and family more than we trust God. To stay the course when we are pressured on every side, God wants us to acknowledge Him and give Him the chance to show himself mighty and strong on our behalf. In Psalms 20:7 (KJV) David says, *"Some trust in* chariots, and some in horses: but we will remember the name of the LORD our God."

When we are feeling empty, God will fill us to capacity if we trust Him as our Maker. God is so awesome and wise. He knows just how much we can take. He is well aware of how our tests and trials should flow. If He dumped everything on us at once, we would drown. For instance, too much water to a plant will rot and kill the plant, and too little water will cause it to dry up and die. God will not suffer us to be tempted above what we are able bear. 1 Corinthians 10:13 (KJV) says, *"There hath no temptation taken you but such as is common to man: but God is faithful, who will not suffer you to be tempted above that ye are able; but will with the temptation also make a way to escape, that ye may be able to bear it."* In this scripture, Paul reminds us that God will not allow His people to be tempted beyond their abilities. There is no temptation that we should feel we are powerless against, because God would not allow us to be tempted by something we could not handle through Him. If we are being tempted, it is something we are strong enough to resist. God is in charge!

Proverbs 3:6 (KJV) tells us to acknowledge God in everything we do, and He will direct our paths. God knows how to organize our day, even when it seems out of control to us. When life seem like it is out of order, understand that God ordained it. We must always choose to stay focused and keep our eyes on God. We cannot afford to miss the shift. If we miss the shift, we will get off course. We must be willing to change directions as God changes our course. Most times, we want to take a route that God has not ordained us to take. When we try to force things, we end up like Solomon and realize that it was all vanity. Even if God has us on a road that does not fit our personality or character, we must trust the Maker and know that He knows the plan He has for you. Jeremiah 29:11 tell us that God knows the plans He has for us! We should not expect to know everything God is doing in our lives. Some things we will never understand until we see Him face to face. God loves us too much to harm us. God is concerned more about us than we are about ourselves. Remember that God's choices are always right. Absolutely nothing catches Him by surprise.

In October 2014, my faith was tested in a major way. I went for my mammogram, and they detected a lump in my breast. The doctor told me that I had to have a biopsy to determine what it was. Well eight years before this, in 2006, I had an abnormal mammogram and found out that I had a mass in both breasts. I had to go for a biopsy, but before I went, I declared and decreed that it was not cancerous. I told the devil that he was trying to invade God's property, and even if God allowed it to be cancerous, I knew He was my Healer. When the results came back, Praise God, it was benign. Now, eight years later, I was facing another abnormal mammogram. This time, it was a small lump in one breast. Once again, I spoke the same words over my body. Deep within my spirit, I heard the Lord say, "You are going to have to go through it this time. It will not kill you. It will be a testimony for my glory." I heard Him speak to my spirit and I had to trust that He had it in His hands.

After I had the biopsy, I had to wait for the results. I already felt that I knew what the outcome would be. The day finally came. On Monday, November 24, 2014, I called the doctor's office to see if the results were in. The nurse answered the phone, and her response put me in a daze.

"Mrs. Viers, the doctor would like to see you in his office. Can you come this afternoon?" she asked.

"Yes, of course," I responded.

At this time, my husband was the only one who knew they had found a lump in my breast. When I called him and told him the doctor wanted to see me in his office this afternoon, his response was, "Oh...boy." I left work to go to the doctor's office, and my husband met me there. I should have been nervous, but I could feel the peace of God in me. I remember telling God, "Lord, if you are allowing me to go through this, I do not want Chemo, and I do not want to be sick." I expressed to God how much I loved and trusted Him because He had made me and He knew everything about me. By the time I got to the doctor's office, I was peaceful and completely confident in God's plan for my life. I knew that whatever happened, I could not afford to allow fear to take over me. I had faith in God, and fear is the opposite of faith. When my husband and I got in the doctor's office, they escorted us to a waiting room. It seemed like it took forever for the doctor to come into the room.

As I sat there and watched my husband, I could tell he was very nervous. I began to pray and talk to him. I let him know that whatever the results were, God had it all in control and I would be okay. The doctor finally came into the room and asked us how we were doing. I could tell he wanted to make us comfortable by starting with small talk, but I was just ready for him to share the results of my biopsy. As he talked to my husband, he fumbled through a stack of papers that were in his hands. Finally, he looked at me and said, "Mrs. Viers, I'm sorry to tell you this. The tumor is malignant. You have CANCER."

The room was silent for a moment. On a real note, even though I heard it in my spirit, I never thought I would have to hear those words spoken to me. The doctor asked if we had any questions and the only question I could think of was, "What do we do now?" He began to explain my options. My next step was to see the chemo and the radiation doctors. I quickly told the doctor that I wasn't going to take chemo. I had already made up my mind. I really thank God for my supportive husband. After the initial shock, he gave me his full-undivided attention to support my needs and decisions. He told me that he would stand with me in whatever decision I made. He encouraged me by letting me know that he believed everything was going to be all right. It is such a blessing to have a saved companion, who you know can get a prayer through!

Now, I had the responsibility of telling my children, family and church family. It was Thanksgiving week, and I did not want to put a damper on everyone's holiday. Also, my son was overseas at the time, and I did not want to alarm him. I begin to pray and ask God to show me how to share the news with my family. I did not want anyone being fearful or negative. I definitely didn't want anyone trying to put me in the grave. After I had told my daughter, I began to encourage her that everything was going to be all right. I expressed to her that I just needed her to stand in faith and be in agreement with me. I reaffirmed that everything was going to be all right. When she finally got over the initial shock, she got a word of confirmation from the Lord. "God's got this!" she shared with me. The war was on.

The one I dreaded telling the most was my son because he was in China. However, I felt I needed to share with him the news before I told anyone else. When he got over the initial shock, he spoke in faith and said, "Mom, you are going to be okay. God is going to heal you."

I waited until after Thanksgiving Day to share the news with the rest of my family. I asked God to help me as I shared it with my family and church family, I did not want doubt, negativity or fear to take control. The Lord directed me to share it with my family one by one. As I shared with them, God gave me the wisdom to speak healing before I even told them the diagnosis of breast cancer. On January 7, 2015, my 56th birthday, I had the lump removed. Glory be to God, they removed the entire tumor! Because of the size of the tumor, the chemo doctor told me I would still need chemo. I stood my ground and declined the chemo again. She wasn't pleased with my answer, but she said it was my choice. I did, however, agree to radiation treatments. I had seven weeks of radiation treatments. Now watch how God works. After they had removed the tumor, they sent it off to the pathologist to see the chances of cancer coming back. When the Oncologist got my test results and went over them with me, she said, "Mrs. Viers, let me explain your test results to you. From looking at your numbers, the chance of cancer coming back is so small, that if I had seen the numbers first, I never would have recommended chemo so strongly. You do not need it!" All the praise belongs to God! This situation taught me that God is still in control, even when we cannot see Him. We must learn to trust Him at all times. Glory be to our God! My beautiful, supportive daughter said to me, "Mom, do you realize in less than five months you were cancer free?" What a mighty God we serve! God is still in charge of my Life!

Through this test, I was inspired to write this book to encourage everyone to just trust God and stay the course!

Saints, if we would only trust God, we will see that He will never let us down! We are living in a time where we use a lot of lip service, but our hearts are so far away. We talk a good talk, we say all the impressive clichés to impress others, but our actions do not match our words. God wants us to trust Him in all things. Staying the Course is a faith walk. We do not know how and when God will fix things in our life, but we must be confident in knowing He is going to fix it. I have been in tough situations. Many times, I didn't see how I was going to come out, but I thank God that I found His Word to be so true! When we cannot see God working in our favor, our faith must step up to the plate and declare that everything is working for our good. Stay the course! Know that God is working things out for you!

Chapter Four
THE POTTER IS AT WORK

"But now, O LORD, thou art our father; we are the clay, and thou our potter; and we all are the work of thy hand."
Isaiah 64:8 (KJV)

"Have thine own way Lord, have thine own way. Thou art the Potter, I am the clay. Mold me, make me, after thy will. While I am waiting, yielded and still." We sing this song often, but do we really believe the words we are singing? It is indeed a beautiful melody, but are the lyrics only words to us? When we can't see or feel the hand of God with us, do we still trust that He is molding and making us? When life goes crazy do we really sit still, wait, and yield to God's Way? Our life circumstances reveal how much we truly trust the Potter.

In Jeremiah 18: 1-6, God spoke to Jeremiah and told him to go to the potter's house. At the potter's house, God would speak to Jeremiah and give him insight and revelation on the condition of Israel. Jeremiah did as the Lord instructed and went to the potter's house. When he got there, he found the potter at work on his wheel. Jeremiah carefully observed the potter and waited on the Lord to speak to him. Jeremiah noticed that the vessel the potter was making was messed up. The Bible says that the vessel was marred, meaning that it was unsightly and messed up. Instead of throwing the clay away and starting with a new ball of clay, the potter took the clay, mashed it back into a ball, and put it back on the wheel again. As the potter worked, the Lord spoke to Jeremiah and said, in so many words, *"Can I not do the same for Israel? Just as the clay is in the potter's hand, Israel is in my hands."*

Israel was in a pretty rough condition. The people of Judah had turned from the Lord. Jeremiah was on assignment from God to speak to the people of Judah about their evil ways. This assignment burdened Jeremiah. Throughout the book of Jeremiah, we can see that the prophet felt discouraged, incompetent, and alone. In chapter 17, Jeremiah cried out to God for an answer about His people. In Chapter 18, God told Jeremiah to go to the potter's house where He would talk to him. The potter's house was probably very quiet, and not very busy. Sometimes, God will cause us to go away from the distractions of our everyday life to hear from him. When Jeremiah got to the potter's house, witnessed the potter at work, and heard from God, he was probably very relieved to know that God could do with his people just what the potter had done with the clay.

I'm not sure if you've ever witnessed a potter at work on a potter's wheel, but it is truly an interesting and unique process to watch. Before the potter selects the clay, he first decides what vessel he will make. Many of our favorite items in our homes are made from clay. The potter decides if he wants to make a cup, a bowl, or some type of decoration. This is important because the use of the item determines how the potter will construct the item.

After the potter has determined the use of the vessel, he then takes his time and selects the right clay. After the clay is selected, it is kneaded with a little water so that it will be flexible and easy to use. Once the clay is flexible, the potter works the clay into a ball. Then, he does what is referred to as "throwing the pot." In this part of the process, the potter throws the clay in the middle of the wheel. The purpose of doing this is to make it stick to the middle of the wheel. If the clay does not stick to the wheel, it could be thrown off as the potter turns the wheel. Next, the potter begins to turn the wheel using the pressure of his hands to shape the vessel and to keep the clay in the middle of the wheel. The potter must be very careful as he spins the wheel. If He spins the wheel too slow, the vessel becomes lopsided. If he turns the wheel too fast, the clay will be thrown off the wheel.

Now that you understand the process of a potter, it may not seem as strange to you that God sent Jeremiah to the potter's house. The same way the potter works with the clay is the exact same way that God works with us. Let's go back to Jeremiah in the potter's house. When Jeremiah got to the potter's house, the clay in which the potter was working with was marred. It was not in good condition. When we find ourselves in difficult situations, we sometimes become marred.

Here's how it happens. First, life throws a hard punch. We pray, fast, and cry out to God for relief. When God does not move right away, we tend to worry and doubt Him. Like the children of Israel, we sometimes find other "gods" to give us an answer or relief. In moments like these, we second guess ourselves and wonder if the course we are on is really of God. These thoughts are planted in our minds by the enemy. He is an expert at attacking our minds. He knows that when we are weak mentally, we won't be focused enough to stand on the word of God. The devil attacks us with low self-esteem, discouragement, depression, and negative feelings. We question ourselves, God, our course, and even those around us. We cry, complain, and become frustrated with everything in our lives. Strongholds are developed, and our imperfections began to show. Even though the enemy meant this to harm us, it still works out for our good. When our imperfections are revealed, the Potter, our great and mighty God remolds us.

The process of being on the potter's wheel is not always an easy one. Sometimes we are left alone. We lose things and people we love. The process does not always feel good, but it is definitely for our good. When God begins to remold us, He fixes everything that was messed up. He works out the lumps, bumps, and uneven areas. Loved ones, if we stay in our Word and on our knees, God will complete what He started in us, and it will be beautiful and perfect. Psalms 119:73 (KJV) says, *"Thy hands have made me and fashioned me: give me understanding, that I may learn thy commandments."* Do you believe in your heart that God's hands have made and fashioned you? Are you willing to wait, yield, and be still while God places you on the potter's wheel and crafts you into the image He has for you? The words "Thy hands have made me" are expressive of the idea that we have been formed or molded by God, as the "hands" are the instruments by which we do everything. Staying the course takes courage because it means we are willing to allow God to mold us in His image. It requires us to trust in His capable hands.

God is all-wise and all-knowing. He knew us before we were even born. He knows everything about us. He knows our purpose, and he understands the path we must take to carry out our purpose. He cares for us and loves us unconditionally. He is faithful to us. He understands that we are not perfect. He knew that when He made us we would mess up. In the midst of it all, God's desire is to fashion us to be more like Him. Each one of us is put on the potter's wheel to be shaped and molded to be usable by Him. We come to the Potter broken in spirit and crying out to Him for help. We don't even realize the pain and suffering we must endure while we are being molded into His image. When we stay the course that God has us on, our lives will begin to take shape into something beautiful. Beauty starts from the inside and works to the outside.

After a potter gets the clay into the position he wants it, he puts it into the fire so that it will harden. Our Potter does this as well. Sometimes, when God allows us to go through the fire, we want to jump out. We feel as though we've gone through enough and that we are complete and ready to come out. No matter what we may believe, we must trust God at all times. We must trust his process and allow Him to control our time on the wheel and in the fire. Often, a partially formed object will crumble into a shapeless heap of clay if it was not properly molded. When we do not go through the proper molding process, we lose vital stuff that is necessary for our destiny. For this reason, we cannot dictate our time on the wheel or in the fire. Romans 9:20-21(KJV) puts it like this, "But who are you, a human being, to talk back to God? "Shall what is formed say to the one who formed it, Why did you make me like this? Does not the potter have the right to make out of the same lump of clay some pottery for special purposes and some for common use?" It is God who makes us, and not we ourselves. We are His people. We belong to Him. We are His possessions and creations. It is not our job, role, or position to tell him how to mold us. We must trust that He knows exactly what He is doing with our lives.

We all are different vessels. We are created uniquely. Not one of us is like another. For that reason, we all require different things on the wheel. We should also bear in mind that the Potter makes each vessel not just to look beautiful, but to also be for the beneficial use of others. My friend, don't rush your time on the wheel. Trust God's timing. He knows just how fast to put us in different situations and circumstances. He knows how long to keep us there. God uses both external and internal pressures in our lives to help shape us. God uses His Word to keep us workable and to make the transitions in our lives smoother. We do not get to tell God how He is to shape our lives or how He will use our lives. Our hearts' cry should always be, *"Have thine own way Lord, have thine own way. Thou art the Potter, I am the clay, mold me, make me, after thy will. While I am waiting, yielded and still."*

Chapter Five
NOTHING CATCHES GOD BY SURPRISE

*"From heaven the LORD looks down and sees all mankind;
from his dwelling place he watches all who live on earth—he
who forms the hearts of all, who considers everything they do"*
Psalm 33:13-15

So many of us have been through and are going through some overwhelming moments. These moments often cause us to ask ourselves, "Does God see what I'm going through? Does He really care about me? If He really cares, then why am I going through so many tests and trials?"

The answer to our question can be found in James 1:2-3. James says to us, *"My brethren, count it all joy when ye fall into divers temptations; Knowing this, that the trying of your faith worketh patience."* The issue among Christians is that we have the wrong outlook on what it means to have joy. We often confuse joy with great health, abundance, and overflow. While these things are great, they are not the basis of our joy. You see, it is easy to smile when everything is going fantastic, our health is good, the finances are on point, our marriages are close to perfect, the kids are healthy, we are working our dream job and the church is flourishing. Dear one, these things are not joy. They are happiness because they are contingent upon what is happening in our lives. What we often view as joy is really carnality because it is based on what we can see and feel. Joy is not based on what we see and feel. It is based on what we know! We can have joy when the rubber hits the road because we KNOW that God is working everything out. We can have joy when tests and trials come from every side because we KNOW that we are already victorious through Christ Jesus. When it seems like we can't catch a break we can have joy because we KNOW that we can do all things through Christ who strengthens us. Joy has nothing to do with what our situations look like. Joy comes from knowing God and His Word! James says for us to count it all joy when we go through tough times, because it is in those moments that we must trust and obey our Maker!

It is beautiful to know that God's eyes are going to and fro the whole earth to keep a watch on His children and show himself strong in their lives. We must be confident that nothing, absolutely NOTHING catches God by surprise. As children of God, we need to come to grips and embrace our tests and trials (which are allowed by God). God knew tough days would come in our life. He knew we would lose a loved one. He even knew we would lose that good paying job. He was also aware that our spouse would walk out on us. God knew in advance about every hardship that we would encounter. Think about it like this: If the tests, trials, oppositions, obstacles, and disappointments did not come, how would God be able to show Himself strong on our behalf?   Stay encouraged by the word of God. Rest in Him. Stay the course. He is making something beautiful out of your life! Trust the maker in all things. His eyes have you covered.

God knows your next move before it forms in your mind. Psalm 91:11-12 (NIV) says, *"For he will command his angels concerning you to guard you in all your ways; they will lift you up in their hands, so that you will not strike your foot against a stone."* That old devil may attempt to hurt or harm us, but he can't! The devil cannot do any more to us than God allows him too. God's Word says that though the weapons may form, they cannot prosper. As you can see in Psalms 91:11-12, God has given His angels special instructions concerning us. He has assigned them to defend and preserve us against the power of the devil's influences of evil. He will not prevail against the children of God that trust in Him. God promised to guard us in all our ways. The path we take must be the path God has us on. God knows everything that is going to happen to us. The moment God places a dream in us, He is the one who sets the day it will be completed. Psalm 147:5 (NIV) says, "Great is our Lord and mighty in power; his understanding has no limit." God has given each of us a path to take. If we stay on the road that has been laid out for us, we will come to our expected end.

As human beings, we have the tendency to fear the unknown. Stay in faith! God will finish what He started in us. God is great and mighty in power! Nothing catches Him by surprise. We must abide in the Word of God. His Word reminds us that the Creator has us in the palm of His hands. We are never out of His sight. God is not going to allow us to figure out His next move. He just wants us to trust in Him. It may not look good today for you, but God isn't finished. God is a God of completion.

When it appears that the plan is not coming together, what do we do? We stay the course! Romans 8:28 (KJV) tells us, *"And we know that all things work together for good to them that love God, to them who are the called according to his purpose."* If you give up, you will never be able to see how God used every storm for your victory! Sometimes, we might experience setbacks when something unexpected happens to throw our plan off course. Do not give up on God! Nothing catches Him by surprise. He knew the Hebrew boys were going to be thrown into the fiery furnace, but He also had a plan for the fourth man to show up. Even when you try so hard to do the right thing and trouble still finds you, that does not mean that God has forgotten about you. He is bringing us to that expected end. Daniel prayed three times a day, but that did not keep him from being thrown into the lion's den. Even though we may do all the right things, we still experience suffering through tests and trials. Daniel had a relationship with God. He did not know how God was going to deliver him from the lion's den, but He knew that God would deliver him. Remember that God's timing is always perfect.

Do not be fearful of life's uncertainties. Learn to surrender everything to God because He will take care of you. Love one, do not fret when it seems nothing is working out for you. Hear ye! Hear ye! We are not hidden from God. We are not out of His sight! He sees, and He knows all things. Remember, you are not a mistake. You are a part of God's plan. We tend to see the smaller picture or one side of the story, but God sees the bigger picture and both sides of the story. Apostle Paul made it clear to us that the storms we may have faced and are facing right now hold no weight that can compare to the glory that shall be revealed in us. The good will ultimately outweigh the bad. Not only that but when we are in God, everything will work together for our good. You cannot lose with God. No matter how bad the situation appears to be, we are guaranteed victory through Christ! Again, nothing catches God by surprise.

Sometimes we feel that the enemy has the upper hand. We might even ask, "Where are you, God?" God's silence does not mean that He does not see what is going on. We have to trust Him at all times. Often, God may allow us to go through certain trials and tribulations longer than others. He knows that if He brings us out too quickly, we might not have that thing out of our system. God will bring us out of a storm, but if we do not get the storm out of us, we will easily revert to our old ways.

When God brought the children of Israel out of Egypt, He took them the long way around. He knew that if He took them the shortest route, they would be afraid and go back into Egypt because the shortest route was a war zone. The Lord did not want them to return to Egypt and the bondage of slavery. God wanted them to go to Canaan, which was to be their Promised Land. He wanted them to acquire the land He promised to Abraham and his offspring. The children of Israel were a stubborn, ungrateful, complaining, disobedient, rebellious, unfaithful, wicked, and stiff-necked people, so the Lord led them around in a circle for forty years. Sometimes, God does the same thing to us.

Instead of murmuring, crying, and complaining about everything, we must remember to give God praise for everything.

God knows what is in us. He knows our heart. God knows how much we can bear. Sometimes, we feel as though our backs are against the wall. We feel that we are trapped. The devil put blinders on us and whispers in our ears, "You are never going to get out of this. You are in way over your head. No one can help you, not even God." In these moments, we must open our mouths and use The Word of God against our enemy, the devil. Just as God fought for the children of Israel, we must trust Him to fight for us too. It is easy to trust God when we remember that ABSOLUTELY NOTHING catches Him by surprise.

Chapter Six
IT'S WORTH THE STRUGGLE

*"But the God of all grace, who hath called us unto His Eternal
Glory by Christ Jesus, after that ye have suffered a while, make
you perfect, stablish, strengthen, settle you."*

1 Peter 5:10 (KJV)

I n 1857, Frederic Douglas delivered a speech that
has echoed throughout history. In his speech he
said, "If there is no struggle, there is no progress."
The word struggle is defined as making forceful or
violent efforts to get free of restraint or constriction.
The enemy comes to distract us with all kinds of doubt
and fear to get our eyes on the struggle instead of the
purpose. The Word of God tells us that after we have
suffered a while, He will make us perfect, establish,
strengthen, and settle us. However, we have a hard
time comprehending the part about suffering! We
want to come out of our struggles as soon as we go
into them. Better yet, we don't want to experience
struggles at all! We look at the scripture above and
wonder how long "awhile" will last. I'm sorry to tell
you this, but there is not a set timeframe for "awhile."
We will go through what God desires us to go through

for as long as He wants us to go through it. God knows how much we can bear because He created us.

Trust me. I understand how frustrating a struggle can be at times. When I moved from Alabama to Indiana to live with my sister and her husband, it was a struggle for me. I was fifteen at the time, and I could not understand why I had to move away from my home. I had lost both of my parents, and I needed a legal guardian to handle my affairs. I thank God that my sister, the late Gladiolus Clay and her husband, (which is now my pastor) Bishop Ernest Clay, gave me a place to live. I could have lived with any one of my siblings, but this was the course God had chosen for me. Back then, I didn't understand, but now, I know it was His plan for me. At the age of fifteen, it was hard to handle leaving everything I was familiar with: my school, teachers, friends and a significant portion of my family. I struggled with this in so many ways, but I'm only going to speak on a few points.

One of the things I struggled with was the language barrier. I was a country girl, as country as they came. Moving to a big city was a major adjustment for me. Can you imagine being teased by other teenagers and adults because of how you pronounced your words and how you dressed? At the time, being different and standing out was hard for me. As a teenager, I did not understand why God had chosen that path for me. It just didn't seem fair.

LEARNING IN THE STRUGGLE

Another issue I had was dealing with shyness and a lack of confidence. When I share with people now of how shy and bashful I was back then, they look at me in disbelief. I've always had the drive to do better and be better, but I did not know how. Through the learning process, God gave me the wisdom to listen to others and how they pronounced their words. I would get by myself and practice words that were hard for me to pronounce correctly.

God is a God of progression. We must stay the course and keep it moving, or we will never be able to see ourselves improve in any area of our lives. The word of God lets us know that we do not have to remain in the shape that we are in, but we must have a mindset to push forward no matter what the conditions or situations might be. We have to take the limits off God and know that God has us on course for His divine purpose.

It is important that we are very careful of the company we keep. We must spend quality time in prayer and God's word. We must make sure that we spend our time around people who inspire us to humbly excel. Often, we learn from the things we have gone through. For this reason, we must stay in tune with God throughout our struggles. Though it may feel as though we are alone sometimes, we are not alone. We have a covering. The Word of God says in Jeremiah 3:15 (KJV), *"And I will give you pastors according to mine heart, which shall feed you with knowledge and understanding."* According to the Word of God, a pastor or under-shepherd is one who oversees, leads, guides, protects, teaches, trains, counsels, preaches, prays with the sheep and for others. While the Word of God says that it is necessary that we go through the struggles of suffering, God designed our suffering to make us perfect, established, strengthened and settled.

BROKEN IN THE STRUGGLE

Research shows that when a caterpillar is enclosed in a cocoon, something happens. Their process in the cocoon is called the Transformation (Metamorphosis) process. Inside the cocoon, the caterpillar digests itself by releasing enzymes that break down it's body. All the components of the caterpillar are liquefied, and the caterpillar becomes soup. If you were to break open a cocoon at the wrong time, nothing but liquid would ooze out. If we compared our lives to this process, this is the time when our will is broken.

God begins to strip us of all the ugliness and pride within us. He strips us of everything that is vain and unpleasing in His sight. During the brokenness, we cry, pray, and many times allow the enemy to get the best of us because we have not yet comprehended that this is only a part of the process. Since we don't understand that it's a part of the process, we fight against it. As our flesh wars against the Spirit, the struggle intensifies because our flesh does not want to die. We want to have our way. This is what makes the struggle painful. One of the main things that have to be broken is PRIDE.

God is not pleased with a prideful spirit because it makes everything about us and not about God. When we are full of pride, God can't use us, so we have to be broken. James 4:6 (KJV) says, *"But he giveth more grace. Wherefore he saith, God resisteth the proud, but giveth grace unto the humble."* When we are being broken, God is teaching us humbleness. When we struggle with pride, we blame everyone for our problems. We point our fingers and blame everyone else for our struggles until we can finally admit that we have a problem. When we can acknowledge that we have a problem, then we can get the help we need.

As we are being pulled in two different directions, this is the time we must know what the Word of God says about being broken. Psalms 34:18 (KJV) says, *"The LORD is nigh unto them that are of a broken heart, and saveth such as be of a contrite spirit."* In the midst of the process of being broken, it often appears that God is so far away. However, the word of God says he is near to us. When we understand that the brokenness is necessary, and humble ourselves under the mighty hands of God, the healing process can begin, and we are strengthened for the next level. It is beautiful knowing that our brokenness is the path that leads us to our blessings.

BEAUTY AFTER THE STRUGGLE

Let's talk more about the caterpillar. The caterpillar's journey begins just like any other insect. It slowly crawls around on the ground with dirt all in its face. Though the caterpillar started out on the ground like other insects, after the cocoon process, it flies so high that the world can see its beauty. One of the enemy's favorite strategies is to make us feel like we are nothing. He desires to make us feel useless and worthless. We may not know why we are experiencing so much trouble and pain on this journey. It is even scarier not knowing how situations are going to work out. Guess what? God has us right where He wants us. He wants us to put our trust and confidence in Him. The word of God gives us the assurance that when God is finished, the beauty starts to emerge for the Glory of God. God takes what was meant for evil and turns it into something good.

You see, a butterfly must struggle to emerge from its cocoon. When the butterfly pushes itself through the tiny opening in its cocoon, this "struggle" moves the fluid from its body into its wings. Without the fight, a butterfly will never fly. God sees us struggling and going through tough times, but He also knows it is establishing us to be an overcomer. God knows if He removed us out of the storm too soon, we wouldn't be able to survive the next test for the next level.

Chapter Seven
ALL THINGS WORK TOGETHER

"And we know that all things work together for good to them that love God, to them who are the called according to his purpose."

Romans 8:28 (KJV)

Typically, we only hear this scripture when we are experiencing something bad, such as the death of a loved one, the loss of possessions or employment, issues with our children, or some type of catastrophe. However, if we actually take a look at it, the Word doesn't just tell us that bad things work together for our good. Instead, it says all things work together for our good.

While we are on this journey called life, we are going to experience good and bad times. The Bible gives us instructions on how to position ourselves as we are being tested. We must remain confident in the Word of God. We must know that if we keep our trust in Him, all things will work out for our good. There are two stipulations that we must take note of: 1. We must love God. 2. We must be called according to His purpose. In this chapter, we will take a look at what it means to love God and be called according to His purpose. Let's begin by reflecting on the story of Joseph.

Many of us have heard the story of Joseph. Maybe you learned about it in Sunday School, or maybe you heard your preacher teach about Joseph's coat of many colors. Regardless of where you heard about it, the story of Joseph is one that is well-known and very inspirational.

Joseph was the son of Jacob. His favor with his father caused him to be hated by his older brothers. Joseph's father gifted him with a beautiful coat of many colors, and this only made his brothers hate him even more. Joseph's brothers grew tired of the favoritism shown to him and decided to get rid of Joseph. Their original plan was to kill him, but Reuben and Judah spoke up, and they decided to sell him into slavery. Joseph went from being a slave, working in the castle, and enduring unfair time in prison to holding a very high-ranking position. Later in Joseph's story, the same brothers who sold him into slavery came knocking at his front door for help. Joseph's decision to help them led him to see the family he hadn't seen in years. You can read the complete story of Joseph in Genesis 35-50. Now that we've briefly reviewed Joseph's story, can you see yourself anywhere in this story?

Sometimes, we are hated or disliked for no reason. As we think about Joseph's story, can we blame his brothers for hating him? Jacob treated Joseph so special because he was the son of his old age. Some of us have experienced favor and grace that causes others to hate the ground we walk on. Joseph nor his family knew the plan God had for them. Many of us are in a place where it seems like God is silent and our life is all out of place. When we spend time with God and the favor of God is upon us, it causes people to shy away from us, or even try to discredit our living for God. Despite how others may treat us, we must remember to keep our confidence in God. Be encouraged and know that all things are working together for your good.

God wants us to walk by faith and not by sight. Sometimes, we might wonder why it seems like some saints can go through life without a care in the world when others go through life with great struggles. That old devil tries to convince us that other people have it better than we do. He even tried to convince us that God doesn't love us and that it is better to live without God. The devil is very cunning and crafty. He tries to make us focus on other people's lives instead of our own. Living God's Word is a powerful tool that gives us confidence in God. Some saints grasp the Word of God and take it for what it says, while others read the same word and still doubt it. The Bible tells us to cast all our cares upon Christ because he cares for us.

Sometimes we experience things that we think aren't fair, and guess what? It might not be fair, but God is fair and just in whatever He does. If we stay the course, we will see that all things will indeed work for our good. Some people are willing to hurt you because they can't connect with what's going on with you, or where God is taking you. Even though Joseph's situation seemed harsh, God was with Joseph every step of the way. Joseph couldn't die because God had him on a path for his purpose.

It might seem like the devil is winning and about to take you out, but unless God says it's the end, it is not the end. We must worship and praise God even in times that are hard. We must delight in His word and know it is going to work out for our good. Joseph was sold into slavery, but everything he learned as a slave helped him when he got into his position! Do not give the devil the power to think he has you down! We must serve Satan notice that he does not have us like he thinks he does! I don't care what your situation look like, go ahead and give God an intentional praise! It is working for your good! God will use your enemy to push you to the next level! However, you must continue to praise God under any circumstances. What the enemy thought would destroy you is growing you! Hallelujah!

God chooses our path, and they are different from each other. We must not compare ourselves with others. Comparing ourselves often keeps us from our purpose. We know that our life is hidden in Christ! Do not fight the path God has you on. Trust, believe, and obey God. He knows what He is doing. I can image that Joseph was comfortable walking and living with his father. I'm sure it felt great to be loved and favored by him. However, God had to move Joseph out of his comfort zone to fulfill his purpose. Sometimes, God must move and break us out of our comfort zone so we can be used for His kingdom. No one likes to be uncomfortable, but those awkward moments break and stretch us to a level of faith that we never knew existed in us until the challenge came to our house. We must trust God with everything within us. We can't see what the future holds for us, but God sees and knows all things! Let Him guide you. He is sovereign. We must trust Him because He knows our ending from our beginning. Once Joseph ended up in the palace, and it seemed like he was catching a break, God still was not done with Joseph. He was falsely accused and thrown into a pit for something he did not do. God was with Joseph because of his faithfulness and integrity. No matter what Joseph went through, he remained faithful to God. In our moments of prosperity or adversity can others around us see Christ in us? Are we still faithful to God?

We are not in the place we are in by mistake; it is where God has us. We must allow God to use us where we are. We can be in a bad situation, but God can still cause us to prosper. In this walk, we will come to roadblocks and delays, but they are necessary for spiritual preparation for our next level. Detours and delays are vital to spiritual growth. It is the place where our faith is made stronger. We learn how to rest, delight and trust God even when it seems that our lives are spinning out of control. Even when people have negative motives against us, it is still part of God's divine plan to make it work for our good. In our lives, we will experience trials and tribulations. This is inevitable. Through it all, will we be able to say that we remained faithful and stayed the course God had for us? Saints of God, be encouraged today. Know that God is working things out for your good!

Chapter Eight
EXPECTED END

"I know the thoughts that I think toward you, saith the LORD, thoughts of peace, and not of evil, to give you an expected end."

Jeremiah 29:11 (KJV)

S in has consequences. The Bible says that Judah sinned against God, and they had to pay the consequences. Sin will never go unpunished. God sent Jeremiah to preach a message of hope to Judah. Judah had to go into captivity for seventy years, but God was going to bring them out. It was a dark and challenging time for the children of Judah. They had been uprooted from their homes, separated from their families, and placed in a pagan land.

Jeremiah came with a message of hope, help, and encouragement right when they needed it the most.

Today, we are in a condition similar to the position of Judah back then. As the people of God, we have drifted far away from our first love. It appears that the Spirit of God is not moving as it was before because we have drifted away in our lust. Psalms 81:12 (KJV) says, *"So I gave them up unto their own hearts' lust: and they walked in their own counsels."* God told His people not to follow strange gods, but of course, they disobeyed Him. He told them He was their God. He told them to open their mouths wide, and He would fill it, but of course, they didn't listen. Therefore, God said that Israel was not His, He gave them up to their own hearts' lust, and they did their own thing.

So many of us are in captivity, and the struggle is real. We find ourselves in bad spiritual turmoil just like the children of Israel. We quote Jeremiah 29:11 because it sounds good to us, but we need to look at why God spoke these words to Jeremiah. Again, the children of Israel were disobedient. All disobedience is sin, and sin will always have consequences. Romans 6:23 (KJV) tells us, *"For the wages of sin is death; but the gift of God is eternal life through Jesus Christ our Lord."* God gives us many chances to repent. He is such an awesome God. He told the children of Israel to live their lives as normal as possible in Babylon because they would be there for seventy years. However, He told them that He was going to bring them out at the appointed time. Jeremiah also told Judah to pray for the welfare of the city which had taken them captive.

The Bible states that our lives should be an example to others. We are instructed to let our lights shine in such a way that the world can see Jesus through us.

Even in our mess, God gives us the opportunity to get it right. Some of us take advantage of God's grace and mercy and choose not to get on the right track. We forget that God will not allow sin to go unpunished. Since God is not a respecter person, He loves us enough to chasten us when we get out of order. When trouble comes to buffer us, instead of getting angry and giving up, we should rejoice that God loves us enough to get us back on track. In Psalms 119:71 (KJV) David says, *"It is good for me that I have been afflicted; that I might learn thy statutes."*

When we are totally sold out to God, we are going to suffer many things. God has given us His word to use as our road map. When fiery darts come our way, we can hide under the shadow of the almighty God. Be sure to read Psalm 91. It is truly food for the soul.

Let's discuss "the expected end". The same message of repentance taught by Jeremiah to the people of Judah is being taught by godly men and women today. They are warning saints to stay obedient to God's Words or suffer the consequences. God did not leave us without a witness, His Word is true. When we are in our good times, we must be careful of how we look at other saints who are going through difficult times. Sometimes, we try to figure out what they have done

67

to cause trials to come their way. We even go so far as to counsel them and give wrong advice. That's why the word of God says in, Jeremiah 3:15 (KJV) *"And I will give you pastors according to mine heart, which shall feed you with knowledge and understanding."* God never designed sheep to lead themselves. He has always given sheep a shepherd. To come to our expected end, we must stay obedient to God's Word and the leadership He places over us. We must be careful of those who say to us, "It does not take all of that to be saved." Matthew 7:14 (KJV) says, *"Because strait is the gate, and narrow is the way, which leadeth unto life, and few there be that find it."* The enemy causes many people to forsake the gift of leadership. Yes, they are human. Yes, they will make mistakes. However, this does not take away from the fact that God has called them to lead us. Don't let the devil deceive you! The Bible says in, Hebrews 13:17 (KJV) *"Obey them that have the rule over you, and submit yourselves: for they watch for your souls, as they that must give account, that they may do it with joy, and not with grief: for that is unprofitable for you."* Can you find one leader in the Bible who didn't mess up (other than Jesus Christ)? Despite all they did, when they repented, God still used them to deliver and rule over many people.

In these times, we must draw closer to God. Things are unfolding right before our very eyes. You may be going through some fiery trials right now, but stay focused and stay the course. God is bringing you to your expected end. He is a God of His Word. If He said it, He is going to do it! When we trust God, it shows in our actions. When we trust God, we praise Him with confidence and power over the situation. Our praise for God will be consistent and persistent when we trust completely in God. We will not be double-minded, doubtful, fearful, or intimidated. We will declare God's word in such a way that it drives the devil crazy. It does not matter who says you are defeated, God's Word says that you are already victorious! Your season is for an appointed time. God is bringing you out! Prepare yourself for the journey and stay the course! It may get rocky, but don't you dare give up! You are coming out!

When God told me He was going to save my children, I did not ask Him for the details. I heard Him deep in my spirit. My life was clean and my heart was pure, so I had no doubt that God was going to do what He said. After God had given me His word, nothing our children did over the next three years looked remotely close to salvation. The devil tried to take their lives, but I declared what God told me about them. I knew they could not die because God said He was going to save them. When God gives you a word, and you speak it, you have just given the devil a pass to challenge the promise God has given you. On the other hand, when God gives you a word, and you keep it to yourself until it happens, you are the only one who feels the effect. When you open your mouth and declare what God told you, do not back down! Keep your praise steady! Remain persistent and consistent in your praise and worship.

Remember that your character is built under pressure. It does not matter who tries to minimize your faith, you believe what God said. When I shared God's promise for my children's lives, someone said to me, "God does not save anyone against their will, and I believe that with all my heart." I didn't allow that to make me doubt God! I knew He was going to do just what He said He would. I didn't know how, but I know God is a promise keeper! But again, keep in mind, I did not ask God for the details. I'm not boasting nor bragging of my strength, but I make my boast in the God I serve! Many times, I had to fall on my knees and cry out to God to give me the strength to hold on to His promise. Many times, I had to put God in remembrance of His Word. Even David cried out in Psalm 25:2 (KJV), *"O my God, I trust in thee: let me not be ashamed, let not mine enemies triumph over me."*

Saints of God, we must stay the course, even when it isn't popular. Sometimes, God instructs us to do things that won't make sense to other people. Do you remember when Jesus told Peter to cast his net in the deep? This didn't make sense to Peter, but he did it and reaped greatly! God will even call us to go to places that we don't understand or want to be.

Following God will cause you to pay your tithes and give offerings when you can barely make ends meet in your home. It may even cause you to turn down a good job for one that doesn't pay enough to take care of your family. What the world doesn't understand is that we can't live the way they advise us to live! We must live and do as God calls us to. It is through Him that we live, breathe and have our being.

If we are to see our expected end, we must follow God's instructions at all costs. Though it may not make sense to those around us, we must remember that we have been called by God, for God. As long as we stay the course and do as he has instructed us to do, we will see everything God has promised us.

Chapter Nine
SOMETHING BEAUTIFUL IN HIS TIME

"But the LORD said unto Samuel, Look not on his countenance, or on the height of his stature; because I have refused him: for the LORD seeth not as man seeth; for man looketh on the outward appearance, but the LORD looketh on the heart."

1 Samuel 16:7 (KJV)

This scripture is often used by those who desire to justify the clothes they do (or do not) wear. However, when we take a closer look at this scripture and the connotation in which it is being used, we see that the Lord wasn't referring to clothes, he was referring to their statute and physical qualification to be the next king. Nevertheless, this verse provides us with some valuable information concerning the outward appearance, but we must put it in the right perspective.

We judge each other based on our outward appearance because that's all we can see. This verse demonstrates that we are indeed visible creatures. While our outward appearance does not mean much to God, it does, however, play a significant role in our testimony to the world. This truth should remind us that as believers, we are always ambassadors for

Christ. How we carry ourselves, talk, act, and live should always be a representation of Christ. People are constantly observing us. We should always be cautious of what we are exhibiting to unbelievers about Christ.

Let's take a closer look at the life of David. God told the prophet Samuel to search for another king in the household of Jesse. When Samuel arrived at Jesse's house, all of his sons were present except David. Samuel looked upon Jesse's sons, saw their firm statues and physical appearances and thought surely one of them would be king. To Samuel's surprise, God had not chosen any of the sons that were present. Samuel proceeded to ask Jesse if he had another son. Jesse informed him that David was out in the fields working. David was summoned, and Samuel took one look at him and assumed he could not be king. Although David didn't look very much like a king, God told Samuel that David was indeed the one He had chosen.

When others looked at David as a nobody, God saw his faithfulness in the field tending his father sheep. Saints, if you want to be used by the Lord, let me encourage you to be faithful where you are. The best thing you can do is to stay the course and grow where you are planted. You must allow God to develop your character, integrity, and faithfulness. God knows where you are and He knows how to bring you to the forefront at the right time. When people count you out, don't worry. Be encouraged in knowing that God sees what others cannot see. He sees your heart. He knows how and when to open all the right doors in your life. Just be faithful and walk with Him. If you would stay the course, He will use you for His glory in His time. It is important that you strengthen your inner man daily by praying and studying God's Word.

Though the anointing of God was upon David as a young lad, he did not take his position as king until much later. After the oil flowed and David was anointed, he went right back into the fields to work. He didn't pack his bags and head to the palace. God still had to develop David in some areas. It's the same for many of us. When we recognize there is a calling upon our lives, it can become very frustrating when God doesn't use us right then. We must be patient and know that He is preparing our hearts for the assignment to come.

While no one was looking, David was being prepared to be a king. He didn't try to push himself to the forefront to be seen by men. He stayed the course of his assignment even though he couldn't see the beauty in it. I want you to take a moment and think about where you are in your relationship with God. Are you able to remain faithful behind the scenes? Are you able to stay the course when no one is looking? I get it. Sometimes it may be unfair to be looked over. Just look at what David had to endure. All of his brothers were invited to the feast, while he was left in the field to work. However, because of the call on his life, David was still invited in God's timing. When he got there, he was anointed as king. I want to encourage you to stay focused on your assignment. It may seem as though everyone else is being picked and chosen in this season. It may feel as though everyone around you is getting blessed, acknowledged, and placed on a platform while you are still suffering behind the scenes. Stay the course! When the timing is right, God is going to bring you to the forefront when you are ready!

My friend, what God has for you is for you. No one can change it. God is looking out for you, even when it seems like people are taking advantage of you. Do not get discouraged when everyone around you is getting married, landing great jobs, moving into beautiful homes, driving luxury cars, and doing everything you could only hope and dream to do.

When God says it's your time, no one will be able to stop the blessings He sends your way.

Sometimes, you may cry out, "God, when will it be my time?" Know that He has not forgotten about you. He knows that you are a faithful tither. He sees you giving generously, making time to help the helpless, visiting the sick, and caring for His people. Even if no one else recognizes it, know that God does. Keep your motives pure and remember that everything you do is for the Glory of God, and not the acknowledgment of men. Colossian 3:23 (KJV) says, *"And whatsoever ye do, do it heartily, as to the Lord, and not unto men."* When we do things unto God, it matters not who pats us on the back, because we know that our reward will come from God. Men can never reward you for what you are worth. Man's reward will always short-change you. However, when we seek our heavenly reward, we know that we will receive beyond what we even desired or imagined.

Another transparent moment would be the time in our marriage where my husband and I did not have enough money to make ends meet. We suffered month after month, and mostly because we were not disciplined in our spending. Our monthly bills exceeded our income by far. We had to rob Peter to pay Paul, but it seemed like Peter never got paid. My husband is a very hard-working man. At one point, my husband worked three jobs, even though I begged him not too. Reason being, I didn't like him overworking himself and it would take away from our family time. I felt like it would show that we weren't trusting God. To each it's own, however, this was my conviction. Being the man that he is, my husband was determined to do whatever it took for him to provide for his family. But guess what? It didn't bring us out of debt but took us further in. I worked as well, but it seemed we just couldn't do enough to make ends meet. I cried out to God constantly because I couldn't understand why we could never get ahead financially. We were living for God, we were faithful to the church, paid our tithes and gave offerings, but we still could not get ahead. One day, I put God in remembrance of His Word, Malachi 3:10 *"Bring ye all the tithes into the storehouse, that there may be meat in mine house, and prove me now herewith, saith the LORD of hosts, if I will not open you the windows of heaven, and pour you out a blessing, that there shall not be room enough to receive it."* As I continued to pray, I asked God when the window He promised would open. When the answer came, I wasn't ready for His reply. He said, "I want you to sow $25 in the offering every Sunday." I was so confused. We already didn't have enough money to pay our bills in the first place. How on Earth did God expect me to sow $25 every Sunday? I didn't understand how God could ask me to give what I didn't have. Can you imagine the struggle? Nevertheless, I praised God and vowed to do just as He instructed me to do. I shared with my husband what the Lord had spoken to me. He was confused as well, but he did not fight against it. He gave me the support to obey the voice of God.

Week after week, I planted our seed of $25. It was a process that required faith and patience. While going through the process, we still went without. Our lights were turned off. We were threatened to be put out of our house because we couldn't pay our rent. Our car was in jeopardy of getting repossessed. No matter what, we stayed faithful to God. It was not a quick turnaround. The Lord had to work some things out of me and teach me how to trust Him even when it did not feel like He was near. I had to repent of not being a good steward over what God had blessed us with. After a year of faithfully sowing the $25.00 seed offering, God opened our window of finances.

Saints, God knows when He can trust us to handle His blessings with a pure heart and not to accumulate for ourselves but to help others. This test was over 20 years ago. I can say truthfully without boasting in my strength or ability that God still has our window of finances open. James 1:4 (KJV) says, *"But let patience have her perfect work, that ye may be perfect and entire, wanting nothing."* God gave me this scripture before we moved to Alabama in 1986. I did not get the full understanding until about ten years later after we went through the test of obeying God to give the $25.00 offering. When God gives us a command, we must be sure to see it through no matter what our circumstances look like. We must be patient and know that once the work is complete, we will be able to appreciate the blessings God sends our way.

Here's a side note. Sometimes in a marriage, both partners may not need the same help in a particular area. Even when it's only one, both suffer because they are one. In our financial situation, it was me who needed the help. I'll be transparent and confess that I was very materialistic. I wasn't selfish by far. Giving to others was a part of my personality. My children had to have name brand everything. I had to get them the latest shoes even when I knew we could not afford it.

80

My husband would always say, "Janet, you know we cannot afford that." So I went out and got a job. That was one of the biggest mistakes I could have ever made. I thank God that He brought me to my senses. I began to listen to my husband. Through submitting my finances to my husband, God brought us to a place where our income exceeds our expenses. I got stuck in the workforce for over 25 years. Through obeying the voice of God and submitting to my husband's plan to come out of debt, I was able to retire at the age of 57. All the Glory belongs to God! If you will be honest and humble yourself before God, He will fulfill every promise to you. That is His word. I'm a living witness that God is faithful. Stay the Course, even when it gets hard. God is making something beautiful.

Let's get back to David. While many of us would have been embarrassed to be anointed as king, but still working in the fields, David did not care at all. He knew he was assigned to care for his father's sheep, and he did it with all his heart. History says that after David was anointed as king, he continued to care for his father's sheep for another ten years. David stayed faithful to God while God was making something beautiful out of his life. As we go through the process of being made usable for the kingdom, we will be tested on every side. We must stay in sync with the timing of God. Sometimes, we will get off track. Our life may even become a mess because of bad decisions and distractions that we've allowed to blur our vision of God. Even in our mess, God still sees something beautiful. He sees a bigger picture. Isaiah 61:3 (KJV) says, *"To appoint unto them that mourn in Zion, to give unto them beauty for ashes, the oil of joy for mourning, the garment of praise for the spirit of heaviness; that they might be called trees of righteousness, the planting of the LORD, that he might be glorified."* Everything will be made beautiful in God's time. Just be patient. He's not done with you yet. Yes, He sees the mess you've made. Yes, He sees that you are off track. However, He still loves you and desires to get you back on track. Sometimes, we must go through a process to become beautiful. When I talk about beauty, I'm not talking about the artificial glamor that the world admires. I'm talking about the real inner beauty that reveals itself in a humble and meek spirit. It will show real character and conduct. God's will is for us to share in the genuine beauty of holiness. If we wait for Him to work, He will bring about that beauty in His own time. True beauty only comes from God. God looks at the heart, and the heart speaks volumes.

In today's society, suicide, eating disorders, depression, drugs, prostitution, adultery, fornication, homosexuality, and teenage pregnancies are at an all-time high. Many of these issues derive from not understanding our value and purpose. So many individuals walk around feeling as if they are not enough. This is only a superficial feeling that comes from the devil. We have been lured into watching television shows and movies, listening to music, and entertaining dating sites and social media posts that do not glorify God. As a result, we measure ourselves against the world's standard of beauty. The world's standard of beauty causes us to focus more on our outward appearance rather than the inner man. While our outer appearance is important, beautifying our flesh is only a temporary solution. After keeping up with the latest fashions and styles, we soon realize that we still won't get the attention we seek, so we move to even more drastic solutions. No matter what we try or do, we still don't feel fulfilled because the true change we need can only come from God. Don't get me wrong, we should want to look beautiful, and take pride in how we look and how we dress, but this should not compensate for the work that needs to be done on the inside. Nothing should take precedence over our spirit man.

So, now is the time for us to get intense and sincere about our salvation with God. We must do this by seeking God with our whole heart. Stay the Course and let God bring out the beauty within us so that it will shine forth for His Glory!

Chapter Ten
NO MATTER WHAT, STAY THE COURSE

"Therefore, since we are surrounded by such a great cloud of witnesses, let us throw off everything that hinders and the sin that so easily entangles. And let us run with perseverance the race marked out for us, [2] fixing our eyes on Jesus, the pioneer and perfecter of faith. For the joy set before Him he endured the cross, scorning its shame, and sat down at the right hand of the throne of God."

Hebrews 12:1-2 (NIV)

Throughout this book, we have discussed many of the situations that cause us to deter from God's path for our lives. As we bring this book to a close, I want you to remember that you are not in this race alone. God has given us His precious Word as well as preachers, teachers, and pastors to feed us with knowledge and understanding. To stay encouraged, we must remember to take advantage of what He has given us. We can't say that we want to be better and do better yet refuse to use what has been given to us.

In the scripture above, the Bible lets us know that we are surrounded by a great cloud of witnesses. The dictionary defines a witness as one who can give a firsthand account of something seen, heard, or experienced. Because we are surrounded by witnesses of God's Word, faithfulness, love, and power, we have no excuses not to run this race God's way. We must be careful not to allow anything to cause us to doubt God or be distracted. We must remember to pray and read His word daily. In this day and time, there are so many ways to interact with God's Word. There are bible apps for our smartphones, many books in our bookstores, and just about anything we desire to know can be found on the internet now. Instead of using the access we have been given for worldly gain, we must take advantage of this access and allow it to aid us in our walk with God.

Galatians 5:19-21 informs us about the many works of the flesh. In this scripture, Paul warns us about the sins that can cause us not to inherit the kingdom of God. In your alone time with God, be sure to read this scripture and ask God to check your heart. If you find that you are guilty of committing any of the sins Paul lists, repent, and allow God's love, grace, and mercy to help you get free of those things.

To stay the course, we must throw off everything that hinders us and the sin that so easily entangles us. We need to throw off things such as, disobedience, the lust of the flesh, the lust of the eye and the pride of life or anything that will draw us away from God. Let us run the race that is before us with determination and perseverance. Let us run this race with confidence that we will reach our goal that is set before us. Let us run this race knowing that when we have finished our Course, we will experience the eternal joy that awaits us.

While on this journey, we may experience times when we feel as if we are not good enough or not capable of doing anything for God in His kingdom. If you read the Bible, you will see that many great leaders, teachers, and prophets also felt this way. For instance, Jeremiah, whom we talked about earlier, felt this way pretty often.

Jeremiah made many excuses as to why he could not do as God had instructed him. He felt like he was too young and that no one would listen. Here's the thing, God knew who Jeremiah was when He called him and gave him the assignment. He was aware of Jeremiah's age because He created Jeremiah. However, none of this stopped God from choosing him. If Jeremiah's age didn't matter to God, then surely his age would have no effect on his assignment. Now, I want you to switch the focus to yourself. What have you been giving God excuses about doing? Understand that God knows exactly who you are. He knows where you've messed up. He knows how much money you have in your account. He knows how smart you are. He knows everything about you. If He still chooses to use you in spite of everything, then who are you to question God's decision? It is not our place to question the path God has chosen for us, however, it is our place to ask God how He desires us to prepare for what He has chosen us to do. So many of us spend so much time whining and complaining that we never start the training necessary for us to be prepared to be used by God. All the time we spend making excuses can be used to seek God's face for instruction and insight about our path.

Another reason we often feel defeated is that we feel as though we have to do things in our strength. Understand that any time you try to do anything in your strength, you will fail. Your desire must always be to seek God's strength to carry out godly assignments. We must stop limiting ourselves and stay before God for the directions for our life. God will ordain us to carry out His every command. God will always equip us with all the necessary armor to stay the course. Again, God is our Creator. He knows all things. Just as

God told Jeremiah, you don't have to remind Him of who you are. He already knows. You have been selected. You have been chosen, and God will not change His mind!

God's thoughts toward us are good. Despite what people have said in the past, God has the final say! You are not a mistake. God made you for a purpose, and if you obey, He will help you see that purpose through. Don't measure yourself by what others say, think, or believe about you. Only God can define you because God is the one who made you! In the same way that Nike can't name a shoe that Adidas made, no one can define you because they didn't make you! That right is reserved for God, your creator. Don't you dare give it away to anyone else.

As I close, I want to encourage you to keep the faith. The word tells us that we will have trials and tribulations along the way, but if we stay close to God, He will lead and guide our paths. God understands what you are going through and God cares. Trust and believe that He will bring you through. My pastor says quite often, "The storms won't last always, the sun will shine again." While we are in the storm, it is hard to believe that we will come out. Our trust has to be in our creator, God. Scream it to the rooftop, I'M

COMING OUT OF THIS. God has provided everything we need to stay on course, but He will not force us to use any of it. God has given us the freedom to make choices. His desire is that we will make the right decision and follow Him.

When you feel distressed, remember Job. Job was an upright man who still had to suffer circumstances that were unpleasant. However, God brought him through because he stayed faithful through it all. Sure, it's easy to rejoice when we can see the end of a thing, but how well can you rejoice by faith knowing that God will bring you up and out? This path we are on is a faith walk. We must walk boldly knowing that God won't let us fall. When we yield our will and ways completely to God, we can be confident that the Lord is working everything out for us! My friend, stay the course! God is making something beautiful out of your life! I love and thank God for each of you who took the journey through this book. I pray that you were enriched through each chapter. I declare that you will stay the course because you know that God is making something beautiful in His time!

Father in the name of Jesus,
I pray that everyone that has read this book is encouraged to stay the course that you have them on. I pray that everyone will understand those words that Solomon wrote in Ecclesiastes 3:1, "to everything, there is a season" meaning that everything we go through will only last for a while. I pray that we understand that no test or trial is designed to last forever. But to everything, there is a purpose under the heaven. Lord Jesus, I thank you for allowing even our tests and trials to have a purpose. I thank you that it is all for your Glory. I pray that we all stay the course until you make the beauty shine forth for your Glory. Ecclesiastes 3:10 (KJV) says, I have seen the travail, which God hath given to the sons of men to be exercised in it. Lord Jesus, I thank you because you see all our struggles, pain, and sorrow. There is nothing hid from you.
Amen.

STAY CONNECTED

Thank you for purchasing *Stay the Course*. Janet would like to connect with you! Below are a few ways you can stay up-to-date on new book releases, book signings, and speaking engagements.

FACEBOOK Janet Lightfoot Viers

EMAIL blessedjv57@gmail.com

WEBSITE www.womenflourishingtogether.org

www.ingramcontent.com/pod-product-compliance
Lightning Source LLC
Chambersburg PA
CBHW072205090426
42740CB00012B/2403